THE MAGIC OF BANANAS

Health benefits, medicinal usages of banana leaves, delicious
banana Recipes, Unique facts about Bananas

ELLE SMITH

ABOUT ELLE SMITH

Elle Smith is a creative personality that believes that creativity can inspire many aspects of one's lives, which is why she is a successful and accomplished artist, designer, poet, cook and has displayed many other hidden talents over the years.

Ms. Smith is exceptionally diversified in her ability to produce conceptual works for her clients with her intellectual strength and an unstoppably innovative right brain. Integrity is at the centre of her work, and so, when you purchase a product made by Elle Smith, you receive something created quite uniquely.

For more unique recipes by Elle Smith, please see her creativity in the kitchen section on the Inspired by Elle website.

COPYRIGHT

Table of Contents

INTRODUCTION

Extensive research has proved that bananas are among the most consumed fruits worldwide. Consuming bananas can help reduce hypertension and lessen the risks of most health issues, which are discussed in this book. Bananas are considered as a mysterious fruit – solely because of the health wonders they perform. The amount of glucose in bananas is relatively high, no doubt – without disputing the fact that the intake of glucose is also paramount to our body system. Therefore, what is the evaluation of banana's overall medicinal nutrients in the body? Are they healthy and balanced or not?

Bananas are in fact an ideal source of organic nutritional supplements, such as potassium, magnesium, dietary fibre, vitamins, minerals, and more. They are mainly the ideal fruit for athletes and individuals that consistently work out because of their quick-acting carbohydrate's influence on our energy degrees.

Bananas are considered as an instant source of energy before an exercise as well as important post-workout nutrients that are required to mend muscle and stabilize water storage. Additionally, bananas contain filling fibre as well.

These added benefits within one 100-calorie chunk of fruit seem so beneficial, but bananas are often complicated for some people, and it's probably not the best fruit option for everyone.

Since bananas comprise of a comparatively high quantity of glucose and carbohydrates (or "carbs"), but basically no protein or nourishing fats, they can increase blood sugar levels instantly. This is difficult for anyone that has any form of insulin protection, as well as people who are pre-diabetic or having diabetes. For this reason, the banana is an effective fruit choice for most people, although not everyone.

If you are energetic and quite proactive, bananas provide a sensible and beneficial food preference to include in your diet plan. However, in case you are hypersensitive to insulin, a problem dealing with blood sugar levels, or have considerable weight to shed, you may opt for other fruit and food alternatives over bananas.

NUTRITIONAL VALUES OF BANANAS

The Mineral and Vitamin Composition of a Banana

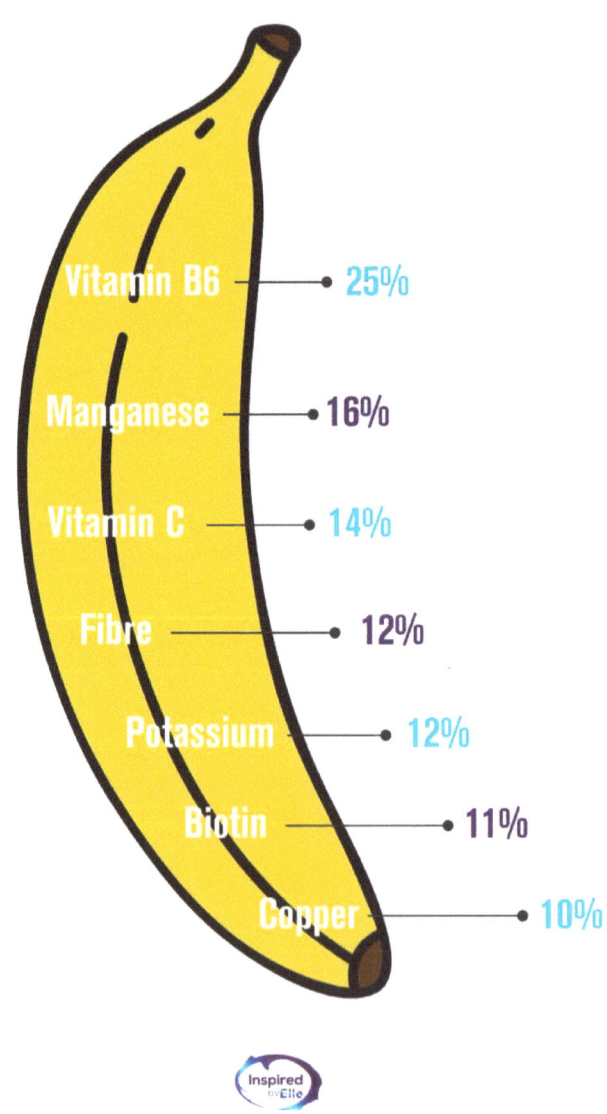

Vitamin B6 — • 25%

Manganese — • 16%

Vitamin C — • 14%

Fibre — • 12%

Potassium — • 12%

Biotin — • 11%

Copper — • 10%

Once you browse through this or other banana nutritional information, keep in mind that they are literally approximations. The nutritional constituents of fruits, vegetables, and other plant delicacies depend on the soil content. Other elements have an effect on the value, as well.

These approximations are often used as guidelines. However, realizing that most of the initial measurements were taken by the USDA years back, there are chances that the nutritional value has decreased.

Virtually all fruits are perceived as the perfect organic, balanced meals we can have daily. The accessibility is endless, and the purposes are effective for the metabolic process. Banana is among the most popular fruits that are preferred almost by everyone worldwide. Aside from being appetizing, the fruit also comprises of lots of high nutrients for amazing health and fitness benefits. Additionally, a banana is easily digestible.

The followings are the details on the nutritional value of the wonderful banana:

Vitamin B6: In 200 grams of banana, you will find 0.6 grams of Vitamin B6. The content is highly effective against bacterial infection. Vitamin B6 also boosts body defense mechanisms.

Carbohydrates: In contrast to most fruits, banana has a greater quantity of carbs. Having said that, the fruit is easily metabolized, and it can supply an immediate source of energy. In 200 grams of banana, it is possible to digest 32.84 grams of carbohydrate, 3.5 grams of nutritional fibre, with 15.23 grams of glucose. In most cases, diabetic people are advised to stay away from banana for quicker outcomes. Most times, they eat other fruit.

Calcium: Calcium plays a crucial part to anything linked to the body composition especially bone and teeth. At the same time, the brain's neurotransmitters equally need enough calcium to function effectively to convey impulses. Muscle contractions also use some quantity of calcium for an excellent purpose. In 200 grams of banana, 10 mg of calcium is present.

Vitamin C: Vitamin C is a fantastic antioxidant that basically provides protection against poisonous and other harmful substances. It can shield the body against vitamin deficiency. In 120 grams of banana, you will find nearly 10 mg of vitamin C.

Potassium: Potassium is a significant constituent that is beneficial for the circulation of blood and thus lessens the danger factor of high blood pressure with the associated health problem. In a medium-sized banana, there is 467 mg of potassium. This is a valid reason for consumption of a minimum of one banana for breakfast.

Other nutrients are fluoride, phosphorus, manganese, magnesium, iron, copper, zinc, and selenium.

Several other nutritional vitamins include folate, riboflavin, thiamine, niacin, Vitamin K, and Vitamin A.

Given these facts, one might assert that the banana has been made available for use naturally to maintain or develop our balanced bodily state. Apart from providing the discussed nutrients, the fruit also helps to resist or ward off stomach ulcers and any related disorders. In certain instances, bananas reduce the chances of diarrhoea.

UNIQUE FACTS ABOUT BANANAS

Bananas are considered one of America's most preferred fruit, with 96% of consumers purchasing bananas a year ago. As a matter of fact, Americans consume more than roughly 30 pounds of bananas per individual, annually. That's fantastic news because bananas are nutrient-rich and provide numerous health benefits. For instance, do you know bananas could actually help you look and feel happy, or perhaps that the scent of bananas can function as an appetite suppressant? Continue reading to find out more about most amazing untold facts about bananas.

1. **The Odour Of Bananas Can Suppress Your Desire For Food**

Bet I have your concentration at this point. Indeed, based on a survey carried out at the Smell and Taste Treatment and Research Foundation in Chicago, perceiving the smell of some food items whenever you are starved could mislead your brain into feeling that you have in reality consumed them. Among those foods was the banana. In case that's not sufficient to persuade you that you could enjoy bananas when reducing your weight, smell one the next time you are hungry.

2. **Bananas Can Boost Your Overall Fitness Performance**

There could possibly be a reason why the majority of the world's greatest bodybuilders and athletes love bananas. Olympian Yohan Blake allegedly consumes sixteen bananas daily! A newly released research from Appalachian State University's Human Performance Laboratory discovered that eating half a banana for each 15 minutes during a biking time test was as effective as having a carbohydrate matched sports drink every 20 minutes. Of course, if you are industrious, bananas are a fantastic means to build up your muscles, and supply deoxidizing substances together with other nutritional value, which sports beverages may lack.

3. **Bananas Are Diet-Friendly**

A relatively small banana is 110 calories and supplies 40 grams of carbohydrates and 3 grams fibre. Together with filling fibre, bananas include repellent starch, a kind of carbohydrate your body cannot break down, but makes it possible to feel satisfied for a longer time. A banana could have 2-3 grams of repellent starch (the greener it appears the more resistant starch it contains). This explains why bananas are an awesome mid-afternoon quick snack, or an ideal pre-workout snack when you consume them an hour before your workout.

4. **Bananas Are Transportable And Easily Resourceful.**

Bananas are an exceptional handy fruit which can be consumed on-the-go or even applied to delicious recipes, from smoothies to baked foods. We are totally convinced that there is not a single banana recipe we ran into that we didn't love!

For a nutritious lunch, alternatively, try this: find some ounces of dark chocolate (over 60% cacao), and melt it. Dice up a banana, and drop each cut in the cacao until the pieces are completely covered. Put them in a container padded with parchment card, and leave it in the freezer. Make sure they freeze and enjoy yourself with a slice as a treat or dessert.

5. **Bananas Supply Vitamin C To The Body.**

It is normally oranges and strawberries that often come to the mind when thinking of a source of Vitamin C, but a plateful of banana supplies 20% of the constant prerequisite for vitamin C. Vitamin C is a major antioxidant that helps counterbalance destructive toxins and keeps systemic swelling under control. They help to generate collagen, which holds muscle tissues, joints, and other tissues collectively. If you would like additional reasons, Vitamin C can help to retain nourishment in blood vessels and is required to optimally soak up iron and folate.

6. Bananas Are Rich In Vitamin B6

Perhaps the popular expression ought to be *"a banana a day, keeps the doctor away."* Bananas incorporate 20% of the daily requirement of vitamin B6. Vitamin B6 lets the body system produce additional amino acids to make healthy body cells. It assists in the production of insulin, haemoglobin and also antibodies that help combat infections.

7. Bananas Supply Relief For GI (Gastrointestinal) Pain

Beginning to feel slightly under the weather? Bananas come in handy because they're easy to eat and assumed to be non- irritating for the digestive system and upper GI region. That's why they are an important part of the medical BRAT food plan -- bananas, rice, and apple sauce with dry grilled toast -- which is a diet plan licensed dietitians recommend to patients experiencing severe diarrhoea. Bananas are among the first weaning fruits that are introduced to children when they start taking solid meals.

8. Bananas Are Rich In Blood Pressure-Lowering Potassium

An average banana yields 422 mg potassium and at the same time it is sodium-free. The excessive potassium-to-sodium ratio can help to reduce the blood-pressure-increasing side effects of sodium in the foods you eat. Numerous researches have shown that those who have meals full of potassium are unlikely to experience high blood pressure and have a lower chance of stroke. Grown-ups require 4,700 milligrams of potassium daily, and thus medium-sized banana supplies practically 10 % of the daily requirement.

9. Eating Bananas Causes Happiness

Think about eating a banana to help you become peachy? A tiny banana supplies 27 mg magnesium, which could aid in boosting one's state of mind. Men and women require 420 mg and 320 mg of magnesium every day, respectively. Low levels and deficiency of this mineral are associated with despair, panic, frustration together with other emotional malfunctions. Since a lot of us don't have adequate magnesium in our diets, consider adding bananas to your daily meal plan.

10. Trick To Ripen Bananas Naturally And Effortlessly At Home

If you are at the grocery store, and every bit of the ripe bananas have been purchased, don't panic. This is a quick tip to make them ripen much faster. Put the bananas in a bag with a whole and unpeeled apple, pear or even tomato. The ethylene gas that those fresh fruits produce fastens the bananas' ripening process. Check them every day until they are ripened to your perfection.

11. Bananas Are Berries

You may be astonished and surprised that bananas are in reality a type of berry. When you look at the meaning of a berry, it basically contributes to the misunderstanding! A berry is considered as any fleshy fruit that originates from the ovary of an individual flower. It has a seed, or sometimes lots of seeds encapsulated inside its flesh. However, have you ever thought bananas don't have seeds? As a matter of fact, they do. The seeds of banana are incredibly tiny that you can't notice them with the bare eyes. Other unusual foods that are classified as berries are pumpkins, tomatoes, and kiwis.

12. Bananas Are Radioactive

Have you ever thought of banana been a radioactive fruit? Don't freak out, this doesn't imply that your health is in jeopardy and you should put an end to eating bananas straight away! Bananas comprise of high amounts of potassium, and it's the K-40 potassium atoms that happen to be the radioactive type. However, the quantity is quite moderate, and humans are in fact more radioactive as compared to a banana as we have non-toxic radioactive potassium in our systems. We must maintain decent potassium quantity in our system to keep them running well. There is absolutely nothing to stress about. You would need to consume 10,000,000 bananas in a single sitting to die from the radiation implications, and that's hardly likely!

13. Bananas Are Not Yellowish In Colour Every time

If you are in the grocery store purchasing bananas, it's certain that you would be checking for the shiny yellow banana colour that is mostly linked to ripeness, and most times, we buy bananas when they are still green, so they can ripen at home. There are several banana types available in the world that are not yellow and yet are edible and yummy. The Red Dacca banana is cultivated in Australia and comes with a reddish-purple layer, so when they're ripe, the flesh becomes light cream pinkish in colour.

14. Humans Possess About 50% The Same DNA As Bananas

Perhaps you may or will most likely not know that bananas share 50% of similar DNA as with humans! However, this doesn't indicate that bananas are our far- away forefathers and consuming them is some sort of genocide. Human DNA is shared with several other plants, microbes, and primates and all living things are composed of the same fundamental component. The primate that shares the largest part of DNA with humankind is the chimpanzee with about 98% of the same DNA chains us.

15. Ripe Bananas Are Beneficial For Weight Reduction

People are often quite mindful about eating bananas when planning to shed weight which is because we link bananas with being a denser more filling fruit, particularly as a single banana comprises of about 35 grams of carbohydrates. Green bananas contain tough and immune starch, which is a type of indigestible carbohydrate ("carb"), but the quantity of repellent starch diminishes as a banana ripens. Therefore ensure you consume ripe bananas as part of a proper diet. Have them at least an hour before your training session to supply your body with the energy it requires for exercise.

16. **Bananas Reduce The Body Blood Pressure**

Overeating salt can easily increase your blood pressure, and research shows that consuming an extra banana generally helps to lower the body blood pressure. Bananas are loaded with potassium, which assists to lessen the degrees of sodium (salt) in the body and reduces blood pressure. It is advisable that an adult's food plan must include 4,700 milligrams of potassium on a daily basis. An average size banana supplies approximately 400 milligrams of potassium.

17. **Bananas Facilitates Ripening Of Other Fruits**

Bananas emit a much larger amount of the gas known as ethylene, which is the hormone that helps fresh fruit ripen quickly. Therefore, in case you have some avocados, peaches or even plums that you would like to ripen faster then keep your bananas in the container with them, and they will accelerate the ripening speed of the other fruits.

18. **Bananas have a general treatment power.**

Bananas are not just an appealing and healthy fruit, in addition, they have the ability to cure and combat some diseases. Apparently, whenever you apply the inside of a banana slice to a mosquito bite attack, the oil in the banana skin reduces swelling and relieves itching. The same thing works for slight burns. The potassium and magnesium present in the banana skin could even help to whiten your teeth. Apply the inside of a banana slice on the teeth for five minutes each night, and you would notice the results in fourteen days. A lot of people report that applying a banana peel on the forehead helps treat a headache, while several others have used banana peel to polish their footwear and silverware.

BANANA RECIPES

1. **Banana Smoothies**

Delicious breakfast power drink!"

Ingredients:

- 0.5 pint of Apple Juice
- 1 Tablespoon of Honey
- 1 Large Banana, in chunks
- 1 teaspoon Vanilla Extract
- 1 tablespoon Icing Sugar
- 0.3 pint of Fiji Water
- 5 blanched Almonds

Method:

This one is absolutely easy – Just place all the ingredients in a blender and blitz away until smooth. Serve immediately as smoothies do not look nice if they are left to stand.

"A great start to the day, or energy boost during the day!"

2. Banana Toasties

"A treat for children young and old!"

Ingredients:

- 2 slices of Bread
- 1 banana, sliced
- Lemon Juice (if you want this less sweet)
- 1 tablespoon Nutella Chocolate Spread
- Icing Sugar to dust
- (You will need a sandwich toaster or even better a Panini press)

Method:

1. Spread Nutella on both slices of bread generously.
2. Then spread the sliced banana on top of the chocolate spread of one slice.
3. Add drops of lemon juice to the banana now, if you want the toasties less sweet. This step is, of course, optional.
4. Sandwich the two slices together, with the bananas in the centre.
5. Toast in the sandwich toaster until golden brown.
6. Remove and slice diagonally into 4 triangles.
7. Serve dusted with icing sugar.

"Simple and yet full of flavour! A great start to the day or energy boost during the day!"

Banana Toasties

3. **Banana Fritters**

"Great for breakfast or snack time!"

Ingredients:

- 2 very ripe Bananas (as in going dark)
- 3 oz. Caster Sugar
- 0.25 pint Milk
- 1 level tablespoon Baking Powder
- 1-2 teaspoons Ground Cinnamon (to taste)
- 2 teaspoons Vanilla Extract
- 4 – 6 oz. Self-Raising Flour
- Extra Flour
- Sunflower oil for frying

Method:

1. Mash the bananas with sugar thoroughly until you have a thick, smooth paste.
2. Add the milk, baking powder, cinnamon and vanilla extract and mix.
3. Fold in the flour until it forms a thick paste, which drops off the spoon with a little resistance (add extra flour if paste is too runny).
4. Leave to stand in bowl until mixture rises up.
5. Place a frying pan with ample oil to heat until quite hot (enough for mixture to bubble if added).
6. Add a spoonful of mixture at a time to form small Pattie sized shapes.
7. Swirl the oil by tilting the frying pan slightly to catch the side of the fritter (to ensure the sides cook).

8. Cook for a few minutes until the underside is a golden colour, indicating that side is cooked.

9. Flip each fritter and cook on the other side.

10. Cook this side until golden, then remove and place on kitchen paper to remove the excess oil.

"Simple and yet full of flavour! A great start to the day or energy boost during the day!"

Banana Fritters

4. **Banana Bread**

"A taste reminiscent of the Caribbean!"

Ingredients:

- 80 mls of Milk, warm
- 1 Large Egg, whisked
- 12 oz. of Strong Bread Flour
- 2 oz Caster Sugar
- 1 teaspoon Sea Salt
- 2 oz Butter
- 1 Large Banana, mashed
- 1 teaspoon Extra Fast Yeast
- 1 teaspoon Vanilla Extract

Method:

1. Place the flour and salt in a large mixing bowl.
2. Add the butter and rub the butter into the flour with the fingertips.
3. Mix in the sugar, stirring well so the sugar is mixed thoroughly.
4. Make a large well in the centre of the mixture.
5. Add the banana, egg, warm milk, vanilla extract and yeast.
6. Mix thoroughly until the mixture is one solid ball.
7. Knead thoroughly for about 30 minutes.
8. Allow the dough to rest in a warm place, covered with a damp tea towel.
9. Leave to rise for about 45 minutes, or until double in size.
10. Knead the mixture again, but this time make into what may seem like couple of giant Swiss rolls.

11. Place each roll into a rectangular baking tin.

12. Allow the mixture to rise, and then baste the loaves with warm water.

13. Bake in an oven at 160 degrees for about 20-25 minutes until golden and hollow sound when you tap bottom of the loaf.

14. Enjoy your loaves with sweet things and savoury as it works for both!

"This bread is a favourite of all family and friends!"

Banana Bread

5. **Banana Soufflés** (Serves Three):

"A delicate soufflé which tastes like it was sent from the heavens!"

Ingredients:

- 1 Large Banana
- 1 Large Egg, separated
- 2oz Caster Sugar
- 1 Teaspoon Vanilla Extract
- 1oz. Ground Almonds
- Butter and Caster Sugar to coat dishes

Method:

1. Using the extra butter coat the inside of three ramekin dishes, and then dust with the extra caster sugar. Set aside for cooking the soufflés when mixture is complete.
2. Take a first of two mixing bowls and add the raw banana.
3. Mash the banana with a fork until no lumps remain.
4. Add the egg yolk, ground almond and vanilla extract to the mixture and beat the mixture with a fork until completely mixed.
5. Place the egg white in mixing bowl number two, and whisk until stiff peaks form.
6. Gradually mix in the sugar to the egg white, adding an ounce at a time and whisking thoroughly to retain as much air in the mixture.
7. Combine the two mixtures in one bowl and fold together until there are no lumps using the back of a spoon and a gentle slicing motion.

8. Spoon the mixture equally between the three ramekins and place on a baking tray.

9. Bake immediately in a hot oven at 150 degrees for approximately 10 minutes.

10. Remove from the oven when the top is slightly golden.

11. Serve with salted caramel sauce and a small jug of cream.

"A very impressive dessert!"

Banana Soufflé

6. **Barbecued Chocolate and Rum Bananas:**

"Sweets are amazing on the barbecue!

Ingredients:

- 6 Bananas, firm and unpeeled
- 6 chunks of Dark Plain Chocolate, good quality 70% cacao
- Some Dark Rum, a few tablespoons approx.

Method:

1. Cut 6 pieces of foil of sufficient size to wrap each banana.
2. Slit each banana in middle, but not deep enough to other side.
3. Place a chunk of chocolate in each banana.
4. Place the banana in a piece of foil, and splash with rum before wrapping up the banana.
5. Bake on the barbecue, turning on each side to ensure the banana is cooked thoroughly.
6. The bananas should take a few minutes on each side, if you have a barbecue going at full strength.
7. Serve immediately on plates, but out of the foil so the rum is not discarded.

"The perfect end, to the perfect barbecue!"

Barbecued Chocolate and Rum Bananas

7. **Banana Crêpes**

"Simple but stylish dessert!"

Ingredients:

- 2 Crêpes
- 2 Bananas
- 1 tablespoon of Caster Sugar
- Juice of one lemon
- 3 tablespoons Evian Water
- 3 tablespoons of Banana Liqueur
- Knob of butter
- Icing sugar to dust

Method:

1. Peel and slice the bananas at an angle into thick sections.
2. Add the butter, sugar, lemon juice and water to a frying pan and simmer.
3. Add the Banana pieces and cook on both sides, being careful not to make them mushy.
4. Add the liqueur when the mixture starts to thicken.
5. Simmer for a few moments, whilst you place the crepes in foil to warm in a hot oven.
6. Serve by adding the mixture to one quarter of the crepe, and then fold twice into a triangle.
7. Pour any excess sauce over the top of the crêpe.
8. Place on a plate and dust with icing sugar.
9. Serve with Chantilly or single cream on a warm plate.

"Impressive but simple to make!"

Banana Crêpes

8. **Fried Plantains:**

"Great for breakfast or snack time!"

Ingredients:

- 2 or 3 Plantains
- Sunflower oil for frying
- 2 oz. of Caster Sugar
- 1 level teaspoon Cinnamon (or to your taste)

Method:

1. The plantains must be ripe in order to fry them this way.
2. Peel the plantains, and slice them lengthwise into slices of about 4 mm thickness.
3. Heat the oil in a large frying pan.
4. Add the plantain slices when hot and fry on each side until golden.
5. It may take longer to cook as these bananas, as they are different to the normal types.
6. Fry on both sides until cooked.
7. Remove each slice as they become golden, and remove excess oil by placing the slices on kitchen paper.
8. Mix the caster sugar and cinnamon, and then dust the mixture over the bananas.
9. Serve whilst still warm.

"These bananas have a completely unique taste!"

Fried Plantains

9. Banana Bakes:

"Run out of bread then you need this recipe!"

Ingredients:

- 1 Banana, mashed
- 1 teaspoon of Caster Sugar
- 1 teaspoon Baking Powder
- 4 fl.oz. Evian Water
- 6 – 8 oz. Self-Raising Flour
- Dash of Vanilla Extract
- Oil for frying

Method:

1. Place the mashed banana, sugar and water in a large bowl and mix well.
2. Stir in the vanilla extract and baking powder.
3. Add the flour and mix into a firm dough.
4. Knead until the mixture forms smooth dough.
5. Divide the dough into small pieces to your taste (ideally smaller pieces are better).
6. Knead each piece into a round ball, and then flatten slightly to about 1cm thickness.
7. Rest the balls on a floured surface for about 15 minutes.
8. Heat a frying pan with ample oil to cook the quantity of balls made.
9. Add each piece and lower the heat to allow the dough to rise.
10. Cook until golden but not brown on the underside, then flip over to cook the other side.

11. The sides may need cooking, so place them as if they were wheels in the centre of the frying pan and roll on their sides until all edges are golden too.

12. Remove and serve, as you would bread.

"Bakes are a great way to use up bananas and provide a nice comfort snack with bacon, or sausages and beans."

10. **Banana Loaf:**

"A treat that everyone will be demanding the recipe for and will be unable to resist!"

Ingredients:

- 6 oz. of Good Quality Butter
- 6 oz. Golden Caster Sugar
- 3 large Eggs
- 8 oz. Sponge Flour
- 2 tablespoons of Vanilla Extract
- 1 teaspoon of Baking Powder
- Grated rind of 1/2 Lemon
- 2 Ripe Bananas – mashed
- 1 oz. Chopped Walnuts
- 4 oz. of Chopped Dates

Method:

1. Cream the butter and sugar until lightening in colour and has consistency of whipped cream.
2. Add beaten eggs to mixture with lemon rind.
3. Stir in sifted flour, baking powder, walnuts, bananas, dates and vanilla extract until well mixed. Check the consistency of mixture is just stiff enough for spoon to stand momentarily.
4. Pour into a greaseproof paper lined 2lb loaf tin.
5. Bake in oven at 150 degrees for 1 hour, check with skewer that centre is cooked if not lower heat and cook for further 5 to 10 minutes.

"Enjoy as this loaf can be kept for a few days, but never lasts that long!"

Banana Loaf

HEALTH BENEFITS OF BANANA

The Health Benefits of Bananas

1	**Potassium**	Potassium-rich foods such as bananas actually offset the effect of sodium (salt) in raising your blood pressure. This, along with a healthy diet and lifestyle, lowers your risk of heart attack and stroke.
2	**Increased Energy**	Sports drinks, energy bars and electrolyte gels are extremely popular nowadays, however you often see professional athletes eating bananas just before and even during their sports.
3	**Improved Digestion**	Bananas are a great source of dietary fibre. A couple of bananas is a better choice than taking a laxative to treat occasional constipation.
4	**Cure for Heartburn**	Bananas are a known cure for heartburn. They help balance your stomach's pH and enhance the protective mucus layer, relieving pain.
5	**Vitamin B6**	Bananas are particularly high in vitamin B6. This vitamin is important for creating hemoglobin for healthy blood.
6	**Skin Conditions**	Even the banana's skin has its uses. It is great for treating skin conditions like psoriasis and acne.
7	**Vitamins & Minerals**	In addition to the high levels of potassium and vitamin B6 mentioned above, bananas also have high levels of vitamin C, magnesium and manganese.
8	**A Cancer Fighter?**	Recent Japanese animal research linked bananas to production of a compound called TNF-a. The potential to increase white blood cell count, thus enhancing your immunity and combating cancerous cell changes.
9	**Reduces Stress**	Bananas are a good source of the amino acid tryptophan which your body converts to serotonin.
10	**Hangover Cure**	Bananas are a great choice for mornings when you've overdone it a bit the night before. A couple of bananas blended with ice, berries and coconut milk or cow's milk makes a really good hangover recovery drink.

Bananas are amongst the most commonly consumed fruits worldwide, together with some of the most easily identified composition as a result of their excellent shape and glowing colour which, combined with the health benefits of bananas, makes them constant in the house. They are nourishing and readily enjoyed uncooked and are usually composed of sugars, like sucrose, fructose, and glucose, in addition to fibre.

For this reason, they are considered as the ideal choice for the supply of energy because they provide both instantaneous and more continuous boosts. There are numerous supplementary benefits of bananas that have been observed lately that could lead to an improved quality of life for individuals of every age group and backgrounds. The conscious intake of bananas helps people to conduct a natural and more vibrant life by benefiting from the vitality and health benefits bananas can offer.

1. **Lowering of high blood pressure:** Bananas are one of the easily accessible food sources of potassium. This mineral is important for sustaining excellent heart function and regulating normal pressure. The potassium in bananas is quite helpful for the kidneys and muscles. Perfect potassium consumption controls calcium excretion in the urine, which would otherwise result in terrible kidney stones. This suppression of calcium reduction also decreases the chance of having osteoporosis and brittle muscles and bones. A banana or perhaps two daily undoubtedly has several significant health advantages.

2. **More Stamina:** Despite the tremendous increase of colourful 'sports' beverages, 'energy' bars with 'electrolyte' pills (which are full of harmful toxins and colouring by the way), you regularly see athletes eating bananas right before and even in the course of sporting activities. Bananas make an awesome snack in the office when your energy is lagging. Bananas might not be the most apparent weight reduction food; they contain about 100 calories allowing it to satisfy those lovely desires. As long as you can substitute chocolate bars and other junk meals with bananas, you

could possibly have a fundamental step concerning losing weight. As an extra benefit, your energy will be much more balanced and uniform.

3. **Cancer Fighter:** Newly released Japanese pet investigation associated bananas which are completely ripe (with the dark spots) to the formation of a compound known as tumor necrosis factor (TNF– a). This compound is a cytokine, which is often assumed to have the possibility to improve white blood cell count, therefore boosting your immunity and fighting cancerous cell variations.

4. **Ambiance Improvement and Lessening Anxiety:** Bananas are an incredible source of the amino acid tryptophan, which the body transforms to serotonin. With several other things, appropriate serotonin degrees help boost your emotion, lessen stress and improve your overall outlook and satisfaction levels. It also helps control sound sleep styles.

Tryptophan is regarded as a vital amino acid because the single way the body obtains it is through your food intake. Bananas, though definitely not the highest source available, are considered one of the easiest methods to obtain extra more tryptophan. One more reason bananas make such an excellent snack for people exhausted at the office.

5. **A Hangover Remedy:** Bananas make the perfect hangover diet for mornings when you have overdone things the evening before. A handful of bananas in a blender with ice cubes, several berries and coconut cream or even natural cow or goat milk formulates an exceptional recuperation drink. Virtually all the other benefits previously mentioned become very important here. Certainly, the best option is never to drink a lot the night before. However, just in case, it's great to have some bananas around for the next morning.

6. **Skin Problems:** Even the skins of this incredible berry have their benefits. Banana skins are applied externally to heal skin issues such as psoriasis and acne. The peeled inside of the banana skin is lightly applied over the infected spot with the remains left on.

This might be best carried out a day in the house or before bed to prevent any banana scent when away from home.

7. **Banana skin is also used to cure warts:** You apply a small portion of banana skin over the wart and then firmly tape it there for a night for at least seven days, probably several, replacing it with a new skin every night.

People in Internet forums have revealed an improvement using these basic therapies, though outcomes with natural remedies may vary.

8. **Good for Ulcers:** Having bananas on a regular basis can help reduce the chances of stomach ulcers. Chemicals in bananas have a tendency to develop a thicker defensive wall in the stomach against hydrochloric acid. Bananas, in addition, comprise of protease inhibitors that basically work to get rid of some harmful bacteria in the stomach implicated as a serious source of stomach ulcers.

9. **Aids Absorption:** Bananas are a wonderful way to obtain nutritional fibre, a substance most of us are deficient. Fibre enables the food you consume to flow easily through the digestive tract whilst enhancing later removal. A handful of bananas could be a much healthier alternative than laxatives to cure periodic constipation. Bananas are likewise known to help reduce the indications of acid reflux. So one more time, try reaching for the 100% natural remedy with banana instead of antacids.

MEDICINAL USES OF THE BANANA LEAVES

Bananas are a highly nutritious fruit but then do they really have any medicinal qualities beyond their nourishing value. Although it may come as a shock to people comfortable with using bananas for cooking, banana splits and little else; extensive research has revealed the whole of the banana plant offers medicinal benefits. Among the properties cited:

• **Flowers:** Used to tackle dysentery, ulcers, and bronchitis. Cooked flowers are known to be the best food for those who have diabetic issues.

• **Sap**: Chemically, the banana sap has astringent benefits. In the medical field, the sap is used to cure numerous health problems, such as leprosy, hysteria, fever, digestive issues, bleeding, epilepsy, piles, and mosquito bites.

• **Roots and Seeds**: Cure digestive irregularities

• **Peel and Pulp:** Clinically proven to include both antifungal and antibiotic constituents. These structures have been described as including the neurotransmitters norepinephrine, serotonin with dopamine.

CONCLUSION

Bananas have excessive nutritional richness. It provides a unique mixture of vitality value, tissue- building constituents, protein, vitamins, and minerals. It is a great way to obtain calories considering that it is loaded with solids and low in water content against other fresh fruit. Bananas are a decent source of Vitamin C which helps to repair the defense mechanisms. Bananas are also effortless to eat as compared to other fruits, and so they are priceless to people with jeopardized immune systems. Vitamin C improves the intake of iron and boosts the production of blood; these two added benefits of bananas make it preferred for people with anaemia or blood-related issues. Bananas could also be combined with a diet plan for high blood pressure as they include potassium, which assists to lessen and regulate high blood pressure. Interestingly, bananas do not contain even quantities of fat, cholesterol, or sodium thereby making it a healthy food alternative for restrictive diet plans.

www.ingramcontent.com/pod-product-compliance
Lightning Source LLC
Chambersburg PA
CBHW040859120626
46551CB00001B/90